How Many Zen Buddhists Does It Take to Screw In a Light Bulb?

How Many Zen Buddhists Does It Take to Screw In a Light Bulb?

Matt Freedman
& Paul Hoffman

?

ST. MARTIN'S PRESS, NEW YORK

Library of Congress Cataloging in Publication Data

Freedman, Matt
    How many Zen Buddhists does it take to screw in
a light bulb ?

    1.   American wit and humor.   I.   Hoffman, Paul,
joint author.   II.   Title.
PN6162.H58   818'.5407   80-13894
ISBN 0-312-39527-2 (pbk.)

To Mom and Dad and Thomas Edison

How Many Zen Buddhists Does It Take to Screw In a Light Bulb?

How many Poles does it take to screw in a light bulb?

Five. One to hold the light bulb
and four to turn the table
he's standing on.

How many Communists does it take
to screw in a light bulb?

Two. One to screw in the light bulb and one to pass out pamphlets.

How many gay men does it take to screw in a light bulb?

Two. One to buy an Art Deco bulb and one to shriek "Marvelous!"

How many Jews does it take to screw in a light bulb?

Three. One to call the cleaning woman and two to feel
guilty about calling the cleaning woman.

How many WASPs does it take to screw in a light bulb?

Two. One to mix the martinis and one to call the electrician.

How many union electricians does it take
to screw in a light bulb?

Seventeen. One to get the light bulb. One to give the
light bulb to the screwer-inner. One to screw in the
light bulb. One to hold him steady on the stepladder.
Four to hold the stepladder steady. One to flick the
switch to test the light bulb. One to make sure that the

other bulbs in the room will need fixing. One to supervise. Two to take a coffee break. One to eat lunch. One to nap. One to plot the best way of breaking into the apartment at night. One to drink martinis with the WASPs.

What's the difference between a pregnant woman and a light bulb?

You can unscrew the light bulb!

How many Californians does it take to screw in a light bulb?

Seven. One to screw in the light bulb
and six to share the experience.

How many Zen Buddhists does it take to screw in a light bulb?

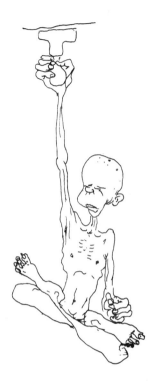

Two. One to screw in the light bulb and one not to screw in the light bulb.

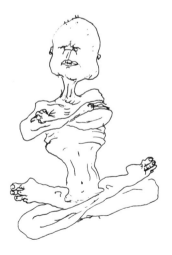

How many Jewish grandmothers does it take
to screw in a light bulb?

How many est followers does it take to screw in a light bulb?

A roomful. They take turns as the leader tells them what rotten and worthless bulb screwers they are. No

one is allowed to leave to go to the bathroom while
the screwing is in progress!

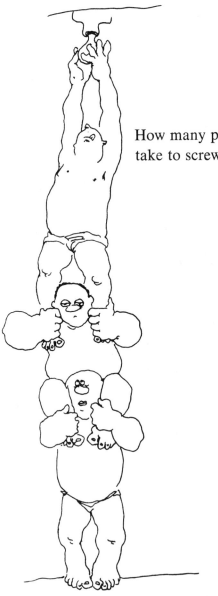

How many pygmies does it take to screw in a light bulb?

Three!

How many lesbians does it take to screw in a light bulb?

Five. One to screw in the light bulb and four to discuss
how it's more gratifying than a man!

How many premedical students does it take
to screw in a light bulb?

Two. One to screw in the light bulb and one to yank
the ladder out from under him.

How many Jewish American Princesses does it take to screw in a light bulb?

What! And wreck my nails?

How many actors does it take to screw in a light bulb?

Only one. They don't like to share the spotlight!

How many Christian Scientists does it take to screw in a light bulb?

One. To sit and pray for the old bulb to go back on.

How many Chinese does it take to screw in a light bulb?

10,000 . . .

. . . to give the light bulb a cultural revolution.

How many mice does it take to screw in a light bulb?

Two!

How many Catholics does it take to screw in a light bulb?

Two. One to screw in the light bulb and one to repent.

How many Democrats does it take to screw in a light bulb?

Two. One to screw in the light bulb and
one to keep his knee from jerking.

How many Republicans does it take to screw in a light bulb?

Four. One to screw in the new light bulb and three to complain about how much better the old bulb was.

How many anarchists does it take to screw in a light bulb?

All of them!

How many Negroes does it take to screw in a light bulb?

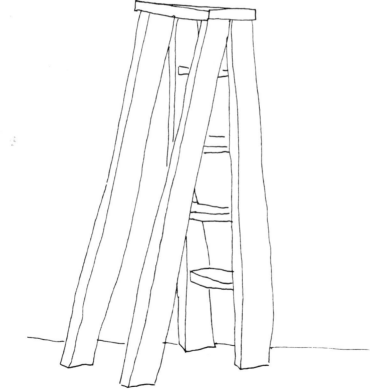

None. There aren't any—anymore!

How many Iranians does it take to screw in a light bulb?

Kho meini! Get it?

No, really.
How many Iranians does it take to screw in a light bulb?

One. But he needs a lot of light bulbs!

How many auto mechanics does it take to screw in a light bulb?

Two. One to screw in the wrong-sized bulb
and one to replace the burned-out socket.

How many college football players does it take to screw in a light bulb?

Two. One to screw in the light bulb and
one to get work-study credit for it.

How many Martians does it take to screw in a light bulb?

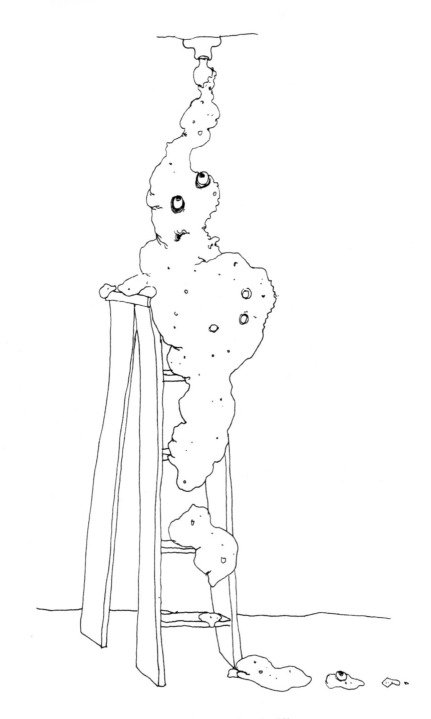

One and a half!

How many Amish does it take to screw in a light bulb?

Amish don't have light bulbs. They bake pies!

How many mystery writers does it take to screw in a light bulb?

Two. One to screw in the light bulb
and one to give it a surprising twist at the end.

How many shaggy dogs does it take to screw in a light bulb?

Fewer than if it were a heavy bulb!

How many nuclear engineers does it take
to screw in a light bulb?

Fifty. One to screw in the new bulb . . .

. . . and forty-nine to figure out what to do with the old one!

How many feminists does it take to screw in a light bulb?

That's not funny!

How many student radicals does it take to screw in a light bulb?

Three. One to screw in the light bulb
and two to insist it be turned further to the left.

How many retarded Italian gardeners does it take
to screw in a light bulb?

One. But don't expect results!

How many television comedians does it take
to screw in a light bulb?

Two. One to screw in the light bulb
and one to shout "Socket to me!"

How many neurotics in therapy does it take
to screw in a light bulb?

One. Three hours a week for five years!

And how many psychiatrists does it take
to screw in a light bulb?

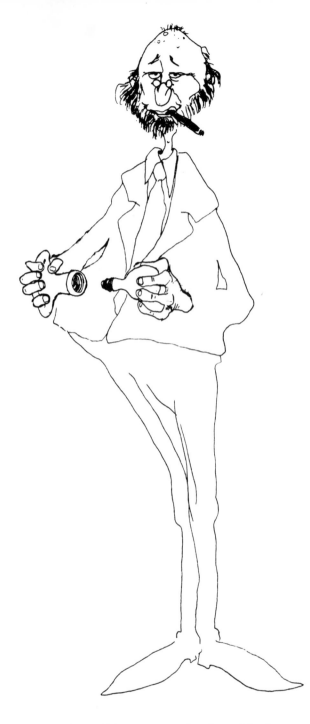

"When did you start having this fantasy?"

How does a light bulb screw you?

Consult your electric bill.

Heard any good light bulb jokes lately?

We'd like to invite you to send them in to us—new ones, or variations on the ones you've just read.

Just send them to:

> MD
> Editorial
> St. Martin's Press
> 175 Fifth Avenue
> New York, NY 10010

Join the newest and fastest-growing joke craze since the **Knock, Knock!**